Dedicated to my mother, who planted the idea and made sure it flowered through, who was the first one to teach me what HR in its essence is all about without even being in the HR business.

1

Introduction

The memoir is basically targeting young professionals of all areas, it is basically a summary of my career life so far which is around the span of 9 years.

All HR related concepts & practices mentioned in the memoir have been studied, explained, & examined by HR professionals as well as academics all over the world, who have more experience and depth and whom we can always refer to for deeper or yet more technical aspects of HR; those are also mentioned in lists as references in this memoir.

The purpose here is to guide young professionals whether in HR or any other domain through the beginning or even mid way through their career and to share with them a real life experience with all its ups & downs.

It is also to challenge them and enlighten them in every possible way.

Chapter One

When I first started to write this memoir, I didn't know where to begin, thoughts came rushing to me and I just couldn't stop them but that also stopped me many times from attempting to carry on with it, I didn't know whether to start with recruitment, my first and major passion, or indulge into compensation & benefits or rather take on explaining the great benefits of Learning & Development.

Then I thought to myself so many great writers before me have really got in depth into such subjects and as a matter of fact are more academically oriented with a massive amount of knowledge and experience.

So I decided I would write about my passion, my day to day business life as an HR professional with the good and the bad, and I assure you the bad exceeds the good on so many different levels, being the department of "Human Remains" as I would like to call it when I am seeing the glass half empty!!

So I sit here in my office, I reached a position where I have an extent of delegation and authority, I can call myself a manager, I have an average sized team of 21 team members and I am in charge of an HR department in a small company with the average head count of 1000 employees, and I am feeling quite accomplished when I am also about to embark on the journey of my 30s.

The company specializes in Retail and is one of the top leading Retail companies in the Middle East.

To tell you the truth this is not what I imagined I would do at this point of my life, I had a plan that I would be an HR Director by the time I was 30, but that was at the beginning of my career when I first started in hospitality and I thought I'd be in a hotel but funny how things change.

I would like to share this journey which took around 8 years for me to get here and I can honestly say it was on the fast track.

I first started as a management trainee in one of the leading hotel companies in the Middle East and to be specific in Dubai, I thought this was a fantastic opportunity to build up my career as an HR professional with all the HR knowledge and the skills that I need to get introduced to as well as the industry knowledge.

Boy, did that turn out to be a blast, we all remember our first job, no matter how fulfilling or not it was with all the ups and downs.

I was enrolled in a program that included all the hotel functions ranging from Rooms Division to Food & Beverage to Housekeeping, I started off at the Sports & Leisure Department and stayed there for a while, had to go through the whole department essentials such as booking tennis courts, looking after the kids' entertainment club and so on, quite enjoyed this part of the program but just when I was about to move to the next department, Food & Beverage, I thought this is not where I would be willing to spend the rest of the year, I needed to start at HR to see how it's being run, so I made the move to the HR department and skipped the rest of the departments.

It's interesting to know that I never studied HR before except for a course or two at university, but the passion was within.

I always thought HR is about interacting with the people, and it sure is, but when I joined the department the amount of paper work to be done was enormous, the intern syndrome started to kick in, by which the feeling of neglect and insignificance hits in yet the drive to prove oneself opposes.

I started to shake it off and got down to business, so a lot of stapling and copying had to take place but that didn't bother me what bothered me was the inability to fully utilize my capabilities and efforts.

One day I was approached by my Manager, so I thought maybe she finally saw something in me and how I proved myself with every task that was given to me, and then she said "I would like you to join me in an interview".

I remember very well my first interview to attend, my Manager was a Filipina and we were interviewing a Filipino for one of the Life Guards positions, the amount of sweat the candidate was sweating was unbelievable I never thought a human being could sweat that much, he started shaking and even asked for a glass of water, couldn't even finish a sentence, I just felt sorry for him, I was just wondering what is the reason behind all this, and then I found out, and I am not trying to judge or be a racist, but there is something about Filipino women that is just intimidating, most of the people who have worked in the Gulf have experienced that, and I came in close contact with it myself.

They are quite organized & sharp, great for administration positions but with minimum people skills except within their own, these are just facts we notice and try not to express out loud but that's what HR is about, taking the good with the bad and trying to understand the nature of your key element "humans".

Back to our candidate, I just felt sorry for him, and I felt even more sorry when he had to cry, later on I discovered this is the Filipino factor and not merely interview related stress, we eventually had to calm him down as he started to carry on and then was able to manage to finish his first sentence, I look at my Manager and she is just interrupting him all the time, eventually he didn't get the position, but I learned something quite important, other than the Filipino factor, I learned I had to be tough during the interview and to investigate like a detective to be able to crack the candidates down and make them confess!! Well, that was wrong!!

I had to sit through 5 more agonizing interviews like these and write down all the questions being asked and then I got to conduct one myself with my Manager present and observing, just like that.

I felt cheated this is not how it should be, I should study more learn more about recruitment, what to be asked what not to be asked, how to tell if the candidate is lying or telling the truth, how to evaluate each candidate against the position they are applying for, how to get it right! Well, I was wrong!!

When I look back at how I got to learn about Recruitment, I couldn't have imagined a better way to do it, and as they say sometimes practice makes perfect and beats academics as I see it really.

That would be my first tip, don't try and make it so academic; every manager should be an HR Manager with all those skills of recruitment, performance management, compensation & benefits, Learning & Development etc.

The set of questions were quite basic ranging from tell me a bit about yourself, to how would you describe a busy day, and where do you see yourself in three years from now.

Here comes my second tip, with all the sophisticated questions and answers to match in the world, if you don't have the skill to read a person correctly then you don't probably have it in you to be a good recruiter.

So I got extremely lucky, I knew how to pick them as they say, and it actually felt effortless.

I studied the questions and I tried not to be as harsh as I was taught, I think it gave the candidates more space to express themselves and show me who they really are.

Some interviews were just bananas that I had to stop myself from laughing so hard that I almost chocked! I remember once I had to interview a candidate who was from India, the poor guy didn't speak a word of English and kept smiling the whole time, I eventually ended up hiring him.

The reason why was because he really was well groomed, kept the smile while I had to burst into laughter at one point, being the young immature person I was back then, and worked in great kitchens back in his country with massive volumes of guests.

I hired him for Stewarding, since he wouldn't have to communicate in English that whole lot with the support of other colleagues down there who speak Hindi, Malayalam and all the languages you could think of.

I am proud to say that this fellow is now a Chef De Partie in one of the worldly famous hotels in Dubai.

I also have to mention the Executive Chef back then, who had the famous phrase whenever we were interviewing for the Kitchen "Can cook then no problem", and he was absolutely right in every sense, the chef is an artist and his language is basically seen and heard on the plate that is served.

Look for the hidden talent and make sure you invest in it, sometimes it would look you straight in the eye with a smile and you will not see it if you choose not to, I highly value that tip.

I went on and on interviewing tons of people for all sorts of positions, I would really have that spark in my eyes every time I hire somebody and that person proves to be up to the level.

I never got tired and being such a multi cultural environment really helped with killing the boredom and routine of doing the same thing over and over again.

I was then introduced to Recruitment Open Days, I really loved going to those events, and I thought it was a great opportunity to mingle with other HR professionals, as well as learn from their experiences and build a network.

At first I thought, "Oh the fun we'll have today", I was wrong!!

We used to interview a thousand candidates per day, it was quite tiring, and by mid day all people would start to look the same and so did the questions too.

I was so scared I'd get that wrong due to the long hours & exhaustion, but the key to this is to always manage to get a break, as simple as that might be, but it is quite essential, so get a break, go for a smoke, have a cup of coffee and make sure you don't skip lunch, I still remember the chats we used to have at these events, we would get so tired that we would start making jokes about candidates behind their backs, to that extent!

However unprofessional this may be but that was a good laugh that would get us through the day.

I had a candidate that I was interviewing, and then he started interviewing me back at one of those events, then I thought to myself how could he, I am the one who is supposed to be asking and not him, I then over the years learned that it's ok to be asked questions as an interviewer and that's not a taboo, you just need to know when to draw the line, and that could be done in so many ways, you could either not respond and carry on with your questions, or smile and nod or even answer a couple of questions without going into details, or in some cases which sometimes you have to, remind the candidate that it is them under gunfire and not you!!

Throughout this period as a management trainee, I was more or less trying to absorb it all and not deviate or improvise a lot, all had to be scripted, the introduction, the response during the interview (remember no reactions whatsoever), the response at the end of it and even the rejection & acceptance letters.

I managed to get by and learn a lot during that process, I also had to go through a whole lot of other HR tasks, so I got to learn about leave, performance appraisals, payroll, training, newsletters, relocation, employee relations, colleagues' rewards programs, and filing (who knew filing could be such an intriguing process!).

I then moved on to a task that I hold close to my heart and cherish, EMIRATIZATION.

I would like to talk about the first point of contact and immersion in that process.

I was the only Arabic speaking colleague in my department and that was an advantage for me, back then in 2006 the country had a target and a vision for Emiratization, so we started applying this on our hotel level and boy was it difficult.

We were set a target of a number of Emirati colleagues that we had to hire throughout the year and in certain departments.

I felt proud to be part of such a project, of giving jobs to the people of the country that mostly relies on Expats for its white and blue collar positions.

I wasn't trained to the does and don'ts of the process, apparently there were many.

I came to learn them again later by practice which again proved to be the best way to do it.

I was given the target with no tools, skills or training on how to achieve it and guess what, I was able to achieve it in the end.

I am not trying to be a hero or look undefeated, but I do believe the reason behind my success, however cliché it may sound, is because I really loved and believed in what I was doing, in the beginning we would meet across the board with all HR professionals who were in charge of meeting the target and discuss the ways of going about it as instructed by our HR Directors.

I was the only Egyptian in charge of this target for our hotel, and that felt good as normally this task would go to an Emirati colleague due to the cultural resemblance and the knowhow but I did it and I enjoyed every bit of it.

We would go onto business trips to the different parts of the country to reach out to and hire Emiratis and later on lots of training programs were in place to rehabilitate this work force and make them able to be productive and efficient in their work place.

One of the negative sides was that you can't push an Emirati candidate to the limit, sad truth, but yes Nationals hold stronger grounds and much more rights in this country far way more than Expats, so you can't really put them to the test or apply the stress interview here, no that wouldn't be right.

Some questions you can't get into and some you can which limits your ability to some extent, furthermore, should the candidate become aggressive or annoyed for any reason, you should hold back and keep your opinion to yourself.

It wasn't tyranny in itself but those were the rules of the game, I guess I wasn't offended or restricted due to the language & cultural advantages, so I went on to recruit some of the most talented Emiratis.

Questions and English tests were part of the process, again the response had to be a little bit softer and nicer, so if you reject, reject nicely and if you don't then be quick and grab them on board to achieve the target and for them not to lose interest.

I have to admit I met some amazing people throughout this journey, the labor market was not sufficient, those are people who were not trained never worked a day in their lives so the skills, knowledge, experience, and language were not there.

We'd get them on board and the training process would start, it was quite amazing how women especially wanted to join the workforce.

It was a taboo for women to work, let alone the fact that they will be working at a hotel with booze & mixed gender swimming pools all around us.

But some of them had to fight their families, some of them had to prove themselves and some would simply not disclose the fact to family and friends that they were working in a hotel.

It wasn't all roses & butterflies, there was definitely a downside to the process, unfortunately and due to being out of the labor market for so long and due to being extremely supported by the government (marriage grants, housing grants, etc.) this workforce is somewhat spoiled.

We had to face a lot of absence without permission or notification, dropping out without a response, ATTITUDE (with the caps on!) and mal performance.

We had to deal with that with a lot of patience, as basically you can't really fire an Emirati that easily.

The key here was building relations with them, the cultural resemblance helped a lot, so it wasn't just about getting them on board, achieving the target and then leaving them behind.

I was there for them and for the department heads all the time; I had to do a lot of coaching, at that early stage of my career, to both parties.

I remember the time when a British Head of Department would come up and really look baffled at how an Emirati colleague just went absent without permission or is just on the cell phone the whole day, thinking "how can this be?" "Is this even possible?" "How can sleeping on duty be acceptable?" "I was just sworn at!"

I then started to baby sit a lot! Until the heads would come to an understanding that it's a process and we all have to commit to, or just leave and slam the door on their way out.

For some case from both sides, it was not going to happen, so still we couldn't let go we would always find alternatives to these colleagues.

However there were definitely stars, people who would shine no matter what, one of them turned out to be a TV chef and yes chef is a lady.

They were just required to be put on the right track and then they really get to fly.

Last but not least and when our hotel finally was about to close down for refurbishment, we had to relocate all active headcount to other hotels within the company.

We were quite lucky to have that luxury and all colleagues had places to work at, the process itself was quite interesting and new for me.

We would first empower our colleagues and give them the knowledge on how to attend an interview, surely we had secure places within the company for everyone but shifting from our hotel to another still required going through an interview.

All the charts, data, coordination came to follow and almost all colleagues secured positions, those who didn't either wanted to move out or wasn't quite interested in what they were offered.

Interestingly enough I was one of the latter; I was offered a couple of positions as an Administrator however didn't see myself in them, I thought as a management trainee and since this was in its essence a fast track management position then I should be offered a better position, since I already proved to be responsible, managed the department on different occasions (when the Manager was away or on sick leave) and got to build a good name within the company.

So I decided to close this chapter, move back to my country & stay in touch with some of the most beautiful people I knew.

Thanks to this rather short period of my life and to sunny Dubai, I was able to know what a team building really means, found out later that donating blood is what we call "corporate social responsibility", and got to understand that HR is everything but Human Remains.

Below is a list of academic HR books to recommend that helped a lot during that period of my life and introduced me properly to HR on an academic level:

- Human Resource Management, gaining a competitive edge, NOE.HOLLENBECK.GERHART.WRIGHT, 5th edition
- Human Resource Management, ninth edition, Gary Dessler

Chapter Two

This next chapter of my life began right after I got home from Dubai, I was a bit disappointed to tell you the truth, I felt I gave so much into the management trainee program and deserved to stay in a position that suited me best but oh well, that led to the next stage which was quite useful as well.

I came back to Egypt and I started looking for jobs, I thought because I just came back from Dubai and due to the "vast" experience I gained through the past year I am going to be a good catch for any employer and shall be hired immediately, well I was yet wrong again!!

I kept looking but nothing matched, the thing is I had very high expectations and those weren't necessarily matching my abilities and expertise but I was determined to find what suited me.

I was really narrowing down my options to HR & the Hospitality industry only and couldn't look or settle for anything else.

I was mesmerized by this industry, its ups & downs and never a dull moment experience.

It turned out that looking for a job at Hospitality & in Egypt wasn't at all easy and that almost all HR vacancies in hotels were full.

Later I found out that hospitality itself in Egypt alongside HR are completely different from what I came to experience in Dubai.

Days went by until one day I got a call from a friend who just knew I was back in Egypt and he told me about this position in HR at a construction company.

First thing that came to my mind was "construction"! I was really into hospitality and wanted to build a career in that industry, remember the dream of becoming an HR Director by the age of 30; that was supposed to happen in a building with a swimming pool, a pub & whole lot of restaurants with different people coming and going!

Then I thought why not, why be stagnant I might like it so I decided to attend the interview and ended up getting the job.

It was a junior position in HR, but was quite good for me to get introduced to HR at the Egyptian market, and get to know the regulations, the only tip here would be, build a good & strong network, you never know when you might need someone or even when someone might need you.

Never lose business cards or delete a cell number off of your cell phone, use every opportunity you get at family events, social events, sometimes when you even are shopping to know more and more people.

My connection, whom I have forgotten about for some time, was the one who recommended me for the job which would start my HR career in Egypt so never underestimate the power of connections & communication.

In Egypt, the concept might have a negative connotation, linking connections to corruption or just getting jobs for people not based on their merit or experience, when it is in that context I would agree, but when it's only to get you recommended or put your name out there, then you do the rest yourself and it's not being forced.

I started the job and started to learn more about construction, was involved in a lot of recruitment open days which didn't differ much from the ones I attended in Dubai, what you know!

What was interesting about this job was the knowledge I gained in the construction field, so I got to know what each position entails and that was completely different from hospitality, all those job descriptions & specifications were quite different as well.

My second tip would be don't merely depend on what is written on paper, when you embark on such a lovely journey of recruiting human beings, it's good to know all the details and specs, these are your criteria for example if you are recruiting an Admin Assistant it's better not to exceed the age limit of 25 and should be a male if that position is based on site, but also get to talk to the people who actually do the job.

In HR, that's the science of Job Analysis, your first step is to create a job description but I prefer to keep it simple, the simpler the better, so talk to your colleagues, spend some time with them, see them in action!

A good plan is to have an induction plan for every new joiner at the company, to get them acquainted with their colleagues & their business partners, that induction plan is quite vital for an HR professional, the person who will most likely deal and interact with all the individuals in an organization.

I call it the enlightening program in our case, HR professionals.

So back to the job, I started to study these job descriptions, job specifications, the policies & procedures of the company.

Until this point, I was not yet deeply involved in the labor law, neither in the Gulf nor in Egypt, however during my period in the gulf, I got to read it but it was nothing compared to the Egyptian labor law.

The UAE labor law is quite simple and not as elaborate as the Egyptian labor law, with the majority population of expats, the rights and duties were quite explicit.

So at that position, I was quite ok with studying the company's internal policies & procedures, and had to do a lot of work on that with my Manager.

My Manager back then was what I like to call hyper active in its raw form, so you can imagine, I actually learned quite a lot from her.

She taught me how to chase things, follow up, & make sure I get things done no matter what.

I just had one thought every time she would be called into our CEO's office, "why does she have to panic like this?"

She used to panic a lot, which also had me thinking this is not how I would like to be one day down the road, it is basically uncalled for and your boss is there to support and not to freak you out 24/7.

I also came to know later, and it was statistically proven in many valid researches, that the first reason why most people leave their jobs is because of their superiors, true fact indeed!

Not in my case, not in this case particularly, she actually managed to keep the whole thing interesting for me, but to a limit.

She believed so much in job specialization, which I am a true believer in, but for a young person willing and eager to learn sometimes that's just not enough.

At least wasn't enough for me, so one day she came up to me and she told me that the company is about to get ISO certified and we need to make sure all is in place to meet the requirements.

So we basically had to make sure that we have job descriptions for all positions within the company, send people on training & document training records, as well as make sure our organization charts are in place, etc.

I was quite happy with the project and gave it my best, but I was just wondering the whole time, why did we have to wait for the ISO to do these things, isn't that the core essence of our job as HR professionals?

We spent hours on all of those things and eventually managed to have everything in place.

My favorite thing was the company organization chart, which is the chart with all positions and the reporting lines within the company.

Until that point I wasn't academically trained as an HR professional, so I wouldn't really know how to go about this.

I just sat down with her, started lining up those positions and basically the reporting the lines followed.

So how do we go about an organization chart from scratch? That was my question.

In my opinion, I would go and sit with everyone at the organization and that is if it's an existing one and not a new one, and talk to people about their jobs as well as their reporting lines, that's how easy it was.

However, for organization charts you need to know how many people will be working in each position, and that was still ok, you just get the numbers of people active in each position, or at least that's what I thought back then.

I didn't know that there was something called "manning guide" where basically you have all the positions an organization would have with the numbers of people to fill them.

Not necessarily to fill all the positions, but to have an estimate for every position while taking the size of the organization, the kind of industry, the kind of work field, as well as the volume of the business & its needs into consideration, and above all that you have to consider your budget as well as the profit you will be making.

That wasn't what I knew, and those are topics that are well researched in so many books but I wanted to see it happen on the grounds.

So eventually we got the certificate, but I reached a point, the point I dreaded since I first started my career as an HR professional, where HR was becoming for me "Personnel" only, that negative connotation of HR, where I am basically a means to archive, file and type.

So I decided to move on, some would think a whole lot of movement especially at this young age and the beginning of my career wouldn't help, I thought the same.

But for me, when the learning & development stopped, I just had to get out of it and look for something else, I always thought, contrary to my convictions, as a recruiter back then, that employers would appreciate my mentality, the energy and what I have to give instead of the numbers of years I spent with some companies.

In some cases that worked and in some it didn't, but I had to move on, maybe it was a generation X versus Y thing!

I also came across colleagues who were just there making it through the day to show up for the next, I called them modern life construction zombies.

I surely didn't want to end up like one and always thought there is so much more that I can give and also take in return.

I quit my job and went on to look for another, however in the midst of all this I decided I would like to take a break.

I thought I graduated and then immediately moved to Dubai, joined the management traineeship program, got back to Egypt and took the job at the construction company, so why not take a short break just to regain focus.

And I did, I travelled a bit and then came back home refreshed and full of energy.

Throughout my experience in HR, I came to learn about this concept, work life balance, and that's quite crucial.

Never underestimate the power of sleep, holiday, a good diet and spending time with family & friends, this is what keeps us going.

I came back and what you know the connections helped again, I spoke to a friend of mine and told her I was looking for a job, she immediately referred me to her superiors and I got the job, after that long enduring interviewing process of course.

It was again an Engineering company, but this time, the company was managing projects in war zone areas such as Afghanistan & Iraq.

The job was great, I was actually given full responsibility of the department, the department that only consisted of one person and that was me!

I was asked to build an HR department and make it work, so I quite enjoyed the delegation and empowerment.

I started looking at different job descriptions online, I started to gather data from the companies I worked for before.

Here I would like to stress that it is very important that you get a wealth of knowledge on paper, if I may say, from all the places you work for.

This is not to copy them, this is to use as a reference, so it is always good to look at different templates, ideas & combine them with your own, it is always good that you come up with your own and you make sure you always do.

I started putting together this data, and I actually started talking to people at the company about their jobs.

I also started putting newspaper ads for recruitment open days, and I had to screen 3000 CVs at a time!

Screening CVs as I was taught was fairly simple, so all you need to do is look for the things you are looking for in a position & person, so you basically look for the relevant experience, the years of experience in each position, the education, the age & location sometimes.

I was also taught that you screen and you short list, and sometimes you create what's called a "Talent Bank", the talent bank is basically your bank of candidates, this bank where you have all the candidates debited and whenever you would like to make a withdrawal, it's always there as a reference.

I firmly believed in the concept, but let me tell you it doesn't always work, you get swamped by all sorts of recruitment channels, and every time you advertise a position you get fresh new CVs that you sometimes tend to over look what is debited in the talent bank.

I try to make it work as much as I can, but sometimes you just can't.

It needs an effort and you need to keep reminding yourself of using it.

All those channels of recruitment, ranging from newspapers ads, online ads, the company website, referrals & walk in candidates helped a lot.

I also was in charge of hiring a colleague for HR to assist, and was quite amazed when my superiors recommended a tennis trainer! Yes a tennis trainer.

This was a family business, and it was custom to refer friends and family for jobs, but a tennis trainer for god's sake.

I had to fight back of course and managed to reject the candidate, I did that because he wasn't qualified and incapable, however I did give him a shot at it and interviewed him but it just wasn't there.

I also did that because I believed I could do it all! Yes you guessed it right I was yet wrong again.

One thing I learned quite early in my career is to keep your integrity even if it means going against the flow or going head to head with somebody, eventually your integrity will get you somewhere and will add value to all the people around you.

I also came to understand that I should never go for the one man show; you will either end up failing or totally consumed that you can't go on another day.

This is how I saw it back then and was determined to do it by myself, I was doing quite ok for a while but then things started to go crazy and night & day started to become a long saga of HR details.

On top of it all, I had to face the labor law and its complications.

I was assigned the social insurance accounts for the whole company, that is basically (as per the Egyptian social insurance laws), to enroll all employees in the government social insurance with the subscription by both the employee & the employer.

So every month, a portion of the salary is deducted from employees' salaries alongside the contribution of the company, quite simple, huh? Not even slightly.

This was a nightmare for me, the social insurance entity in Egypt is well known for its extreme bureaucracy and red tape.

So I thought I'd rather visit one of those social insurance offices and see things for myself and I did.

All those rumors about those places were merely sugar coated and far away from the truth.

I went in there and it was hell on earth, paper everywhere, two or three people sitting at one desk, people having breakfast on their desks, & everything was just horrific.

I kept on making these visits, until I got an idea about the whole process and started filling out the forms, & sending them to the social insurance office, etc.

So basically, there are two main things to do when you are handling social insurance, first is to make sure you fill out (form 1) for all new joiners and you fill out (form 6) for all leavers.

You get to review this every half year while checking (form 2) to make sure all your active staff members are socially insured and the leavers are out of your company's account.

Forms 1 & 6 are illustrated by the end of this chapter.

Still I wasn't able to grasp the amount of routine that had to go into filling these forms out, especially when I would make a visit to the office to enroll employees in or take them out of the system.

It was always daunting for me, I still remember how some employees at the social insurance office were just rude & unhelpful, and how the manager there refused to help and left it all within the subordinates' control.

Then later on and not during this stage, I found the secret out, and it was quite simple, bribe!

It's a sad truth, but to make your life easier at these places, all you have to do is give a little here and there to make sure things are run smoothly, you will not even have to follow up that much and everything will be done for you like a king or a queen for that matter.

I am glad I didn't know that back then as it forced me to go through the whole process & absorb it from top to bottom.

So I was working day & night, looking at ways to improve the department, and ways to manage performance appraisals, attendance, as well as medical insurance.

That was all quite satisfying until one day I got a call from the past.

It was my ex-company in Dubai calling me for a position that just came up at one of its resorts and they thought I would be interested.

It felt so good, they remembered me, and it has been almost a year, and they did call me back.

I didn't hesitate, I loved that company and had a great sense of loyalty to it, and this company was where I first knew what HR was all about.

I took the call and was offered the position of an Assistant HR Manager.

I was quite happy to move back to that company and to sunny Dubai.

Below is a list of academic HR books to recommend that helped a lot during that period of my life and introduced me properly to HR on an academic level:

- Management- the new workplace, Daft/Marcic
- The seven habits of highly effective people, Stephen Covey
- Below is an illustration of form 1 &6 (social insurance forms)

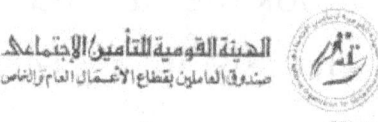

الهيئة القومية للتأمين الاجتماعي
صندوق العاملين بقطاع الأعمال العام والخاص

نموذج رقم (١) قرار وزاري رقم (٥٥٤) لسنة ٢٠٠٧

منطقة :
مكتب : ....
وحدة : ....

طلب
باشتراك مؤمن عليه طبقا للقانون ٧٩ لسنة ١٩٧٥

رقم المنشأة : ☐☐☐☐☐☐☐☐☐☐☐   قطاع المنشأة : ☐
اسم المنشأة : ....

بيانات المؤمن عليه

الرقم التأميني : ☐☐☐☐☐   الحالة الاجتماعية : ☐☐☐☐☐☐☐

الرقم القومي : ☐☐☐☐☐☐☐☐☐☐☐☐☐☐

اسم المؤمن عليه : ☐☐☐☐ / ☐☐☐ / ☐☐☐   تاريخ الميلاد :

الجنسية : ☐☐☐   المؤهل : ☐☐☐

كود المهنة للمؤمن عليه : ☐☐☐☐ / ☐☐☐   المسمى :

تاريخ بدء الاشتراك : ☐☐☐☐ / ☐☐ / ☐☐

نوع المدة :   المسمى : ☐   كود الاشتراك : ☐☐   المسمى :

الأجر الشهري الأساسي : ☐☐☐☐ جنيه ☐☐ قرش   القطاع : ☐

الأجر المتغير : ☐☐☐ جنيه ☐☐ قرش

صلة القرابة بصاحب العمل : ☐   * تستوفى للأقارب حتى الدرجة الثانية بالمنشآت الفردية

بيانات العجز إن وجدت : تاريخ بداية العجز : ☐☐ ☐☐ ☐☐   نسبة العجز : ☐☐ %

بيانات محل إقامة المؤمن عليه

عقار رقم : ☐☐☐☐   شارع / حارة :

ساحة / قرية : ☐☐☐   قسم / مركز : ☐☐☐   محافظة : ☐☐

توقيع المؤمن عليه : ....   توقيع المدير المسئول : ....

تحريرا في :   /   /   تم مطابقة التوقيع بمعرفتي : ....

البيــــــان	مستلم الطلب	المراجـــع	سجل آليا بمعرفة	روجع آليا بمعرفة
الاسم				
التوقيع				
التاريخ				

ملحوظة : على صاحب العمل والعامل الاطلاع على التوجيهات الموضحة خلف الاستمارة مع التوقيع على الإقرار.
(اسطر خلفه)

الهيئة القومية للتأمين الاجتماعي

صندوق العاملين بـ ....
منطقة : ....
مكتب : .... وحدة : .... □□

إخطار بإنتهاء اشتراك مؤمن عليه

رقم المنشأة : □□□□□□ مسمى : ....

بيانات المؤمن عليه

الرقم التأميني : □□□□□□□□

الرقم القومي : □□□□□□□□□□□□□□

الاسم : ....

تاريخ إنتهاء الاشتراك □□□/□□/□□ سبب انتهاء الاشتراك □□

بيانات محل إقامة المؤمن عليه

عقار رقم : □□□ شارع / حارة : ....

شياخة / قرية : □□□ قسم / مركز : □□ محافظة : □□

إقرار المؤمن عليه والمدير المسئول

أقر أن البيانات بعاليه صحيحة وأن المؤمن عليه تسلم صورة من هذا الإخطار.

توقيع المؤمن عليه .... توقيع المدير المسئول .... ٢٠ / /

تم مطابقة التوقيع بمعرفتي /

إقرار المدير المسئول في حالة وجود نزاع

أقر أن البيانات بعاليه صحيحة وإنني أرسلت صورة من هذا الإخطار إلى المؤمن عليه بخطاب موصى عليه بعلمه الوصول برقم .... بتاريخ / / ٢٠

خاتم الجهة

توقيع المدير المسئول / / ٢٠

البيان	مستلم الاخطار	المراجع	مسجل إلى	مراجع إلى
الاسم				
التوقيع				
التاريخ				

ملحوظة : ـ يلزم التأكد من توقيع كل من العامل وصاحب العمل على الإقرار الموضح خلف الاستمارة.

Chapter Three

This chapter of my life I highly cherish, that was the period when I moved back to Dubai around the beginning of 2008.

I can honestly say that this was when I learned the most both on a professional and a personal level, those two are inseparable "professional & personal", they do have an impact on each other big time.

I moved back with all the hope and the energy in the world, I was thrilled about the position being an Assistant HR Manager with the immense focus on recruitment, my first and major passion.

Recruitment, can truly affect performances of organizations up to making money and winning awards.

It's the starting point, where all of what you see later in an organization begins.

I went back to Dubai and worked for one of the biggest resorts in the company (the same company I used to work for before I moved back to Egypt).

That was a resort that held an average of 3500 employees and conjoint 3 hotels as well as a souk "shopping & dining area".

Everything looked familiar, even the people, it was the same company, the same rules, even some of those colleagues that got relocated from the closed down hotel for refurbishment (remember from the first chapter!).

It was also great to go back to Hospitality, my first home & mentor.

I had to go through the same cycle of induction and training as to when I first started with the mentioned resort, but it was all quite exciting for me.

It was good to see that within two years, the programs have changed and new trainers have joined the business.

I was then able to join HR, and was quite familiar with all the processes & procedures.

That's what struck me, the procedures, policies, formats, and even interview questions were the same.

The company did so well on the training level but lacked on HR, which is quite close to the concept of HR as being stagnant and not adapting to neither the organization nor the industry changes & needs.

I started the process of recruitment and it was quite enjoyable, the thing is it was always volume recruitment.

We had a headcount of 3500 colleagues with sky rocketing turnover ratios, so we had to keep on filling those vacancies.

Turnover rates were so high due to managerial issues, where managers weren't supportive to staff members, discriminative, selective when it came to long working hours and poorly performing on the reward side.

Then there were the other reasons of benefit packages, new hotels opening in the region, people just wanting to go home and settle, etc.

The process itself though was magnificent, I got to go into details of so many new positions, I also got to hire managerial staff members and that was an upgrade for me, career wise.

One day I had to hire a Reservation Manager, everyone was having quite a difficulty finding someone for that position, the hours were crazy and not really matching the compensation package, but I was able to finally find her.

She was a British Nigerian candidate, who lived most of her life in the UK and had great reservation experience.

She fit perfectly and she matched all what we were looking for and to be honest we were just tired of looking, but still she was on a scale 1 to 10, a 9.

We were happy to get her on board, however before that process started, the candidate kept calling me and asking about her benefits, etc.

At first, I was glad to answer all her questions and walk her through the process, as this was the first time for her to become an Expat in a Middle Eastern country.

Then there were a lot of negotiations regarding the benefits, which I was happy to meet almost half of them, and she was happy too with the outcome at one point.

However it never ended, and she kept coming back to me with all those questions & objections, then my gut feeling started to kick in, when you know you just know.

I started to feel that she is not really into it, and due to poor judgment on my side and trying so hard to fill that position, I shook my gut feeling off and kept convincing her to join the resort.

She eventually joined, and everyone was quite happy with her performance, but surprise surprise she didn't last in the position for three months!

I was crushed, really was, since it was one of the first managerial positions I was recruiting, but then got to value my gut feeling, that would be one of the most valuable tips I share "never let go of your gut feeling, if it tells you something wrong then something is wrong".

During this period of time, we'd get together as a team and update each other on the vacancies filled or not and for what reasons, as you can imagine what the volume was, so regular updates had to take place.

It was the first time for me to encounter such update meetings as well as morning briefings.

Constant communication is key and can drive the whole organization better.

One of the things I appreciated about my boss at that time was her flexibility and eagerness to learn, every week she would ask me and my other colleague (Recruitment Coordinator) to pick a hotel chain from around the world and do some research and then we'd sit together and discuss.

Great names came up during these discussions such as Banyan Tree, Dusit Thani, Starwood & many others.

Got to know more and more about hospitality and how other hotels operate, great times indeed!

During that period, I got to know what psychometric tests were as well as assessment centers.

Those are sets of questions that would get deeper into a candidate's abilities & personality.

I always believed that a face to face interview is much more valuable and is the greatest determinant, but those tests were there just to further support & make the process evident, especially for more senior positions.

I also came in touch with the recruitment software, and this was helpful big time, saving all your CVs online, responding to candidates online, advertising for vacancies, having an online talent bank and even generating reports.

Emiratization was still part of the territory and I was in charge of it and all what it entailed at the time, the same concepts of recruitment and training applied since I was first involved in the first hotel.

But then the financial crisis hit us, and it was time to let people go.

One of the very emotional & hard times we all had, in fact the whole country had at the time.

People were let go in volumes around Dubai, leaving their cars (bought on loans) in the airport, it was madness.

Back at the resort, we were asked to start the sacking process and we did indeed, I was one of the lucky ones, since all recruitment was on hold and we had even to let people go, that recruitment focus was removed from my day to day responsibilities and I just had to focus more on HR.

I welcomed the challenge, and didn't see it as a change actually.

I do have to mention that one of the great values that I grasped while working for this company was one of its principles "Never say No to a guest", this principle brought the idea of flexibility and before you say no, why not try and find alternatives, you never know what might come up or what you might achieve.

However, that principle sometimes got the best out of me, I wasn't able to say no to anything, so I overloaded myself with so many things, never turned a request down so again I would go back to the "one man show".

Personally this turned out to be one of the most excruciating times of my life.

Everything was going well in the beginning, and the concept of HR Business Partnership was just introduced to the resort.

The concept was about being a champion and looking after all HR related issues in terms of recruitment, performance management, employees relations, etc. for certain functions at the resort.

The concept was also about taking initiative and going to the colleagues instead of waiting for them to come to us.

Oh the number of disciplinary meetings I had to attend ranging from sexual harassment charges to theft (and yes the money was kept in their socks & underwear!!), the bizarre things I had to witness...

However, during this period I would like to dedicate more time to office politics, I had to learn about that but the hard way.

I would like to share this with the fresh hires out there in the world, office politics explains it all.

While I had to focus on HR due to the downsizing of recruitment, the whole team was different and much more competitive.

Competition is always healthy; it brings out the best in us as long as it is clean.

Turned out to be the opposite in this case, just before the crisis we had a couple of new HR Directors joining the department.

As the time went by, things started changing; people were promoted within the department with no proper justification, and employees of a length of service with the department as well as great performers, were passed over for new joiners or even people with mediocre performance.

All based on the type of nationality, it was very unfortunate but it was the truth, a lot of racism was going on in that place however nobody was watching to rectify or take action.

It wasn't very late until it was my turn to catch up with the gang and be affected.

One of our Senior Directors, one whom was very fond of my performance and was a major reason why I wasn't let go during the financial crisis turned out to be a micro manager with a defensive hat.

She would pick on everything I do, even the way I dressed, she was against everything I had to say, professionally and personally even if it was right.

I'd go into meetings and my opinion would be shared with others, I could see that she agreed with what I was saying and she eventually ended up taking my advice and went by it, but during meetings and in front of everyone else she had to say I was wrong and I wasn't up to any good!!

Work became hell for me, every day I would get up in the morning and think what would she have for me today? It was daunting.

As time went by, I came to know that it was the other HR Director who joined at the same time she did, who was behind all this.

At the beginning she wanted to get so close to me, we even became friends and went for each others' dinner parties.

The circle of trust, as we were taught in both our personal lives & professional lives is quite important.

If there is no trust, then things will surely fall out of order at some point.

The thing about the circle of trust is that you have to enter it with grace or else it will be a trap, and that was the case.

The more we became closer at work and other wise, the more tension dominated the relationship with our Senior Director.

Things got worse with the Senior Director and I eventually had to submit my resignation, it was the first time for me to leave a workplace due to such reasons, being not able to cope with my superior.

At the time, Dubai was still suffering from the financial crisis and Abu Dhabi was booming, lots of people moved from Dubai to Abu Dhabi where a lot of vacancies were coming up, as well as new hotels.

So I figured and considering what I was going through at work, that I should look for something on the other side of the country and I did.

I did get a position at a Telecommunication company in the HR Department and that was late 2009.

I was not quite happy since I had to leave the hospitality industry again and more specifically, this company, where I first got to know what

HR is about and had a great team with different people.

But it was time to leave, I wasn't the only subject to discriminatory acts and such treatment, so many colleagues, unfortunately outside of the European spectrum, were treated even worse and had to leave.

So I left and came to know only after leaving the company, that the person behind all of this was the person I trusted the most and was friends with.

So many people left the department, and surprisingly enough the Senior Director whom I had the feud with left too.

People either left and went on to join other hotels within the company or left the company altogether.

One of the very few who stayed and is still there until now is the HR Director who was supposed to be my "buddy"!!

I went to Abu Dhabi, and felt the difference between the two Emirates, Dubai was so young, hip & fresh, everything was moving so fast, Abu Dhabi or at least for me wasn't.

I had to move, but again and most importantly my gut feeling was against this move, but I lost the battle again and surrendered to my final decision to move to Abu Dhabi.

The holding company was huge though however the company I was assigned to was quite small, and the team was wonderful, I still remember them, I still remember my boss who was one of the most supportive people I ever came in contact with.

The package was great and the relocation went smoothly, much better of a process than when I was in Dubai.

But something kept saying at the back of my head that I just committed "career suicide", it wasn't hospitality, and the company was small as well as not very well known in the market.

Days went by while I decided to make my job matter; I was again the only person in HR and had to work on improving the department.

Previously, the department was just personnel, so basically administering leave, attendance & payroll.

I came in with all of those ideas, to start workshops for formulating the job descriptions, job specifications and the whole ten yards of recruitment standards.

I also was in charge of performance management, employees' relations, payroll, personnel, compensation & benefits & training.

It was exciting to build up the department like that.

During that time, it was the first time for me to encounter audits, so we had an audit committee coming from the Head Office to audit our files and everything, a couple of months later when I joined the company, how lucky!!

The committee checked all the personnel files, which I went through when I first joined so phewww, that went well and I was lucky indeed!

The thing I learned about Audit is never panic, because just the concept of someone looking through your stuff with the intension to find mistakes, and I assure you they come in with that intension full speed, just makes you panic even if there is nothing wrong.

Look at it, as your mentors, auditors are meant to find gaps and that's why we have them.

To improve and work on their recommendations as well as better secure our processes.

The other exciting thing I worked on was handling performance management, the only drawback about my boss was that she didn't really encourage conflict however healthy and productive it might be and wasn't a good advocate for confrontation.

So she dumped all of that on me, one of those times I had to fire a colleague who just joined the company, I was mainly looking after the HR Department for the company in Abu Dhabi but I had to manage the other two HR Departments in Egypt & Lebanon from time to time.

So I had to fire a colleague working for the company's branch in Lebanon and it was tough.

He wouldn't let go of the position, was quite rude and was a lousy performer to tell the least.

We couldn't sack him and I eventually had to go to Lebanon on a business trip to sack him and finally managed to get it done.

One of the interesting situations I had to face was that I discovered that one of the employees is registered in the company and is on a residency however doesn't work for the company.

This employee was actually a current employee's spouse and held the Palestinian nationality.

At his place of work he wasn't able to get a residency so the EX- HR Manager granted him a visa so he could continue his presence at the country without facing the threat of being deported and carry on within his current job at another firm.

Here I was taught the importance of review and spot checks, never underestimate the power of follow up, random spot checks and careful reviews especially in a career like HR.

I always admired the saying that we, as HR professionals, are the gatekeepers of policies & procedures.

During that time, I was also glad to get involved in the area of residencies at the UAE, simple process in my opinion but was good to know the does and don'ts of it, as well as the details it entails.

All of that and it was yet again time for me to leave again, I wasn't attached to the company and really wanted to go back to hospitality and kept hearing that voice at the back of my head that it was indeed "career suicide" so I did it and I came back to my home country Egypt, saying good bye to sunny Dubai & Abu Dhabi and closing that chapter in my life of being an expat.

I was determined to go back to Egypt and start a career there, it was time to settle down in one place and lessen the movement a bit, as well as get into the Egyptian market.

Below is a list of academic HR books to recommend that helped a lot during that period of my life and introduced me properly to HR on an academic level:

- The HR value proposition, Ulrich/Brockbanck
- The boundaryless organization: breaking the chains of organizational structure, Ron Ashkenas, Dave Ulrich, Todd Jick, and Steve Kerr

Chapter Four

The next chapter of my life begins in Egypt, where I just came back from Abu Dhabi.

This time I was in full speed, looked at things differently and was determined to make it in Egypt.

It turns out perception is all there is, the way you perceive things is the way you will shape your life, funny how the brain works and how thoughts can really shape your day to day life as well future.

I didn't want to take a break for long, and stayed in touch with the company back in Abu Dhabi, so I was basically doing consultant work for them but remotely.

I was the one who built the department up so they regularly referred back to me for different cases.

I started looking for jobs and since I was mortified by the idea that I just came back to life from the "career suicide" I committed as I mentioned in the previous chapter, this time I was determined to only look for jobs within the hospitality industry.

It has always been my dream to join a hotel's pre-opening team and start things from scratch.

So I did narrow down my options to pre-openings only, and I went on looking and looking.

I was able to locate a job online, working for a pre-opening in a remote province in Egypt "Sharm El Sheikh" so it was time to relocate one more time.

It's worth mentioning here that online ads form a good source for recruitment, so my tip here would be to really look through all online ads and post your CV on all the websites & blogs possible, you never know who will be interested in your capabilities.

Blogs are also a nice channel for building a network and getting to know different HR professionals & practices throughout the world.

I took a chance and applied for the job and travelled to the property itself for an interview.

I met with the HR Director who walked me through the property, which was still under construction.

So basically the role would be building the department up from scratch, what you know dreams do come true!!

He also had me go through some of the tasks that I would be handling, this is called Realistic Job Preview (RJP), a well known approach to get candidates in touch with their jobs before they start.

So candidates are faced with their real jobs and expectations to avoid any misinterpretation or unmanaged expectations later on.

It was a well known Spanish company that had all sorts of boutique, luxury, business, and leisure hotels around the world.

I accepted the role immediately without thinking twice.

Pre-opening does require previous experience in HR as well as knowledge as it is a build up process and here I would like to be detailed about what I was in charge of doing.

I took the role of Assistant HR Manager, directly reporting to the HR Director and managing a team of around 6 people.

So it was the first time for me to be in charge of a whole team and indulge into direct people management.

I basically started putting together job descriptions for all positions as well as constructing the manning guide as well as the salary surveys/scales & handled recruitment for all positions within the hotel.

I managed building up the administration part of HR so I started up an HR Administration Manual, a Recruitment Manual as well as SOPs (Standard Operating Procedures).

I had to then construct all the forms & templates that were the outcome of those manuals.

And then after the hotel was opened, I was in charge of all the department's expenses as well as turnover, training, & recruitment reports.

That also came with the territory of compensation & benefits, reward system & employees relations.

Until now I haven't been seriously involved in budgeting which is something that is quite important and every manager even in the beginning of their managerial positions should be aware of.

It is all about Profits & Return on Investment (ROI) by the end of the day.

I was massively involved in training and inducting new employees.

Training has always been a passion of mine but not like HR in general.

I always found it refreshing and rewarding, I wasn't really educated academically as a Trainer but had the skills.

As a Trainer, you have to have the passion for passing on the knowledge in a way that all minds grasp.

And you have to know your material well and be an Entertainer instead of just a Trainer, in the sense that the training you provide should be amusing and catchy no matter what the material is.

I was also involved a lot in the labor law and its applications, so at the time I started getting in touch with how performance management is handled within the framework of the Egyptian labor law.

The law in that sense and others is much more sophisticated than the Gulf and to be more specific the UAE labor law.

The Egyptian labor law and as I view it, is on the tipping scale of favoring the Egyptian employee over the employer.

Where you have all these rights; simply as not being able to fire somebody easily & not after a series of investigations, warnings in addition to a committee being assembled to reach the final decision.

Employees could easily file complaints against employers in government labor offices and be rewarded even during falsification of events some times.

So I had to study the labor law so well and most importantly I had to practice it a lot.

This hotel was amazing in every sense; these remote locations basically depend on labor force from provinces other than the capital

Cairo and even have certain exceptions in the labor law like annual leave for example.

So I had to come in contact with the different mentalities as well as cultures.

Working in a multicultural environment is such an experience, in the UAE I had to come in contact with so many different nationalities, working in such work frame you have to be a bit careful as to different cultures and customs but the similarities are vast, after all we are all human beings.

In Egypt and where I was working the majority of employees was from Egypt but from different parts of Egypt which gave the hotel its depth.

I was becoming quite familiar with the labor law and its applications.

Even an employee file has to be a certain way according to the Egyptian labor law, so there are certain formats that need to be filled like the history of leave applications, this basically is to track employees' leave days and make sure that employees go for leave as stated by the labor law.

Being an HR professional in Egypt, merely and basically depends on a deep knowledge of labor and social insurance laws.

If you master that, then you master the whole game.

This also comes with years of experience, as the law has many gaps & tricks that you have to master.

I know HR professionals who have been in the HR business for so many years in Egypt and still referred to books or other HR professionals for support & queries.

So always have the labor law & social insurance law latest editions saved on your desktop or placed at your office, they come in handy mostly.

Always have a network of well experienced HR professionals as well, people who have practiced the law on the grounds and came in contact with different cases.

All was going well until the Egyptian January Revolution erupted in 2011 and there was a travel ban to Egypt, so tourism was hit to the core and hotels' occupancy levels really dropped down.

I had to relocate back to Cairo as I was genuinely concerned about my family and couldn't really leave them behind during that period of time.

The revolution and the stepping down of the Egyptian president at the time went on until the month of February 2011 and after that period Egypt went through a "hold phase".

Everything was on hold, unemployment is quite high in Egypt but after the January Revolution the rates sky rocketed and some investors had to leave the country due to the turbulent political & economic situations.

Some new investors had to put on hold or withdraw their investments as well.

That was a rough time both for employers & employees, whereby some companies had to close down, or go through a downsizing process.

This is the period that I like to call "Career limbo" and would talk more about in the next chapter.

Below is a list of academic HR books to recommend that helped a lot during that period of my life and introduced me properly to HR on an academic level:

- Six thinking hats, Edward De Bono
- Leadership, great leaders.great teams.great results, Stephen Covey

Chapter Five

And now with the moment we have all been waiting for ladies & gents, I present to you the career limbo.

One of the toughest career moments of my life, the January Revolution was at its beginning, that was in 2011 and everything was on hold.

The massive gatherings & demonstrations ended in February 2011 however the country was in a transitional period and safety & security were big issues.

Most companies put recruitment on hold and in the aftermath of it all; some companies just opted to close down or downsize to say the least.

Hospitality was not even an option at that stage of time; there was a travel ban to Egypt that went on for quite some time.

So there was no chance there, this didn't mean that I didn't try to work for hospitality, I actually did but all the doors were closed.

So I started looking in other areas and didn't really mind, it was important to get a job and get things moving again.

So I started looking everywhere, this time and as recommended by so many friends, I went knocking door to door for a job!

Everyone was saying forget about referrals and online job postings, it is a tough time and you have to get out there and find yourself a job.

So I did and I printed my CVs in dozens and I went on knocking all doors.

I wasn't quite welcomed mostly, there were times where I had to wait for an hour just to submit the CV as the receptionist didn't accept CVs and the only department entitled was HR and the person in charge wasn't around for that matter.

Until one day I was successful and I got an interview in an English Training Centre, so you can imagine how things went.

It has been 6 months of job search and I was ready to throw in the towel, so I accepted the position.

I had to go through a series of preparation to be able to conduct this sort of training, although I have been a trainer before but not a language trainer, so there is a set of skills to be acquired in that arena.

I can't say it wasn't helpful, I actually learned a lot.

I started to conduct sessions for junior levels and I then moved on to teaching intermediary levels.

I was then nominated to conduct training for advanced levels and even for students preparing for the TOEFL exam as well as university professors who wanted to enhance their language skills.

All was ok, but of course and as clear as it was I wasn't quite happy so I didn't really last long in that position.

I carried on till I finished all the sessions required and never bailed on a group.

Training is such a joy, when you see the effect on people, knowledge is power and that's for sure.

But I had to move on, I spent around 3 months in that position, and the country was on its way to stability & the job market was about to reopen.

I started applying here and there, until one day I got an interview at a training academy.

It was an academy being launched in cooperation with the Japanese Cultural Centre in Egypt and they had all sorts of training courses to offer.

So what do you know, back to Training again, it was interesting how every time I applied for a position in HR nobody would take me and I would only be accepted in Training positions.

I went for the interview and got the job, but this time it was neither in HR nor in Training!

It was actually a job in Business Development, which merely was sales, so they were basically looking for a well presented colleague to go on and sell those training courses to different entities.

I accepted with great hesitation, but it was worth mentioning here that I was asked to prepare a slide show about training in general.

It is very important to have those skills as well as the skills of public speaking.

Public speech doesn't come easily, it just needs continuous practice and I was able to finally grasp it.

However I still get nervous when I have to do a public speech now and then, the key is to be well prepared and just take it easy, forget about the audience while you are presenting.

I didn't really stick around in that position, as soon as I had to go through the realistic job preview later on and got to know what the job was really about, I immediately left.

At first and when I first asked, I thought I would be a trainer but then it turned out to be a position in Sales.

At some point, I even tried to customize training courses and have a free lance career, but the market was down and wasn't really receptive to paying money for training at the time.

I also wasn't up to that expertise to construct such training courses; I only wanted to construct very simple basic ones.

So I started applying for jobs again, until I received a phone call from one of those holding companies looking after a bunch of hotels, furniture stores, car dealers, etc.

It was an HR position, so I thought oh finally the moment is here.

I went for the interview and I got the job, but it's worth mentioning here, that I didn't land every job I applied for.

I am only referring here to the jobs where I was accepted and I am writing about the experience I gained from such work places.

However I was rejected so many times and even for jobs I was just the right fit for.

This didn't bring me down though and those were only stepping stones in my career life; being introduced to different interviewing techniques and companies' backgrounds was quite helpful.

That was an HR Manager position, and I was looking after a couple of colleagues, in Egypt the term "micro manager" is actually quite normal and dominates work places.

I guess this has to do with the fatherly figures or it's a cultural thing, or maybe it has to do with the majority of the work force being nationals.

Unlike Dubai for example, where most of the work force are expats and bound by visa, a market where nationals dominate is a bit different to operate, even in the UK.

Nationals tend to be more relaxed and labor laws as well unions are by their side.

So abusing sick leave for instance is common, where as to expat dependable job markets the case is entirely different.

In Egypt, and to add there is the cultural factor of being sentimental so when you, as a manager, opt to fire somebody, you are immediately demonized & that somebody is immediately victimized.

All of that combined led to the micro manager concept; managers trying to control more than delegate, in order to keep the flow going well.

So the majority or at least the managers I worked with in Egypt are micro managers.

I actually think that this type of management actually works in Egypt but for some characters not all.

It didn't work for mine at least; I am pro delegation and empowerment.

I started working for this company and it was again time to build up another HR department!

The boss was one of the greatest men I have ever come in contact with, despite being a micro manager.

He was such a great guy, with a great sense of humor and great knowledge of the Egyptian labor market.

He was also well rounded when it came to Egyptian labor and social insurance laws and was really committed in his position.

Everyone liked him and he was 100% there for everyone.

This time I was also going to be more involved in the labor law and its applications however that didn't last long and it was very difficult for me to leave just because of that great boss!

I was approached by one of the companies I once applied for in the past few months.

That was an international Retail company and one of the main Retail companies in the world.

This is where I am right now, however for ethics sakes I will not get into details about that for now.

However I can honestly say that I am proud to be a part of such a great organization.

I really came out of my comfort zone and was delegated to do things I would never think of doing or coming across in my career path.

Below is a list of academic HR books to recommend that helped a lot during that period of my life and introduced me properly to HR on an academic level:

- Why the bottom line isn't: How to build value through people and organization, Dave Ulrich and Norm Smallwood
- "From partners to players: extending the HR playing field", Dave Ulrich and Dick Beatty